To Jerry,
With love, Anna
December 14, 2005

GREECE

LAND OF LIGHT

With best wishes

Nicholas Gage

Jan 1, 2000

GREECE
LAND OF LIGHT

TEXT BY NICHOLAS GAGE
PHOTOGRAPHS BY BARRY BRUKOFF

A BULFINCH PRESS BOOK / LITTLE, BROWN AND COMPANY
BOSTON NEW YORK TORONTO LONDON

WE DEDICATE THIS BOOK TO THE INDOMITABLE SPIRIT OF THE PEOPLE OF GREECE.

ACKNOWLEDGMENTS

For his continued interest in my photographic endeavors through the years, I thank Jim Silberman.
For their invaluable support in the preparation of this book, my thanks to Janet Swan Bush, Sandra Klimt,
and Heather Brook Graef. For their efforts in providing assistance to me while I traveled in Greece,
I thank Alexei Revides of the Greek National Tourist Office, Dimitri Coromilas, Mixos Saliveras, and
Demitri Manesis. For their vision and acumen, thanks to Morrie Camhi and Owen Edwards.
—Barry Brukoff

TEXT COPYRIGHT © 1998 BY NICHOLAS GAGE
PHOTOGRAPHS COPYRIGHT © 1998 BY BARRY BRUKOFF

FIRST EDITION

LIBRARY OF CONGRESS CATALOGING-IN-PUBLICATION DATA

GAGE, NICHOLAS.
    GREECE: LAND OF LIGHT / TEXT BY NICHOLAS GAGE; PHOTOGRAPHS BY BARRY BRUKOFF.
    P. CM.
    "A BULFINCH PRESS BOOK."
    INCLUDES INDEX.
    ISBN 0-8212-2524-3 (HARDCOVER)
    1. GREECE—CIVILIZATION. 2. GREECE—ANTIQUITIES. 3. GREECE—PICTORIAL WORKS. I. BRUKOFF, BARRY. II. TITLE.
    DF741.G34   1998
    949.5—DC21   98-13212

FOR INFORMATION REGARDING INDIVIDUAL PHOTOGRAPHS, YOU MAY WRITE BARRY BRUKOFF CARE OF
BULFINCH PRESS, LITTLE, BROWN AND COMPANY, 3 CENTER PLAZA, BOSTON MA 02108.

DESIGNED BY BARRY BRUKOFF WITH HEATHER BROOK GRAEF

BULFINCH PRESS IS AN IMPRINT AND TRADEMARK OF LITTLE, BROWN AND COMPANY (INC.)
PUBLISHED SIMULTANEOUSLY IN CANADA BY LITTLE, BROWN & COMPANY (CANADA) LIMITED

PRINTED IN HONG KONG

Previous page: THIRA, SANTORINI

GREECE

THRACE

MACEDONIA

• EDESSA

• THESSALONIKI

• KASTORIA

MOUNT ATHOS
•

MOLIVOS
•

LESBOS

• PAPINGO

EPIRUS

• LIA

CORFU

• METEORA

• IOANNINA

THESSALY

PARGA
•

SKIATHOS
•

ALONYSOS
•

SPORADES

SKOPELOS
•

SKYROS
•

PIRGI

CHIOS
•

MESTA
•

PIRGI
•

CENTRAL GREECE

IONIAN
ISLANDS

NAFPAKTOS

• DELPHI

EUBOEA

ATHENS
•

AEGEAN ISLANDS

KORINTH
•

OLYMPIA
•

ARGOS
•

PELOPONNESE

NAFPLION
•

AEGINA
•

CAPE
SOUNION

TINOS
•

MYKONOS
•

PATMOS
•

ANDRITSENA
•

DELOS
•

HYDRA
•

CYCLADES

PAROS
•

NAXOS
•

KALYMNOS
•

MISTRAS
•

SPETSES
•

SIFNOS
•

NAOUSSA
•

VATHIA
•

MONEMVASIA
•

FOLLEGANDROS
•

OIA
•

SIMI
•

RHODES
•

THIRA
•

ARCHANGELOS
•

KYTHIRA
•

SANTORINI

DODECANESE

RHODES

LINDOS
•

N

↑

CHANIA
•

HERAKLION •

KNOSSOS
•

CRETE

PHAESTOS
•

OIA, SANTORINI

CONTENTS

On my first visit to Greece in the mid-1960s, I recall climbing the hill of the Acropolis and seeing the glowing marble of the Parthenon. Alone on that hill overlooking Athens, I felt some deep inexplicable connection to this land. I spent only a week there, but knew I would return.

When I did return a dozen years later, I felt an overwhelming sense of coming home. How was that possible after merely spending a week there? I was told Athens had changed quite a lot and I would be well advised to head for the islands, where this book began to take shape. I returned every year to travel, to explore new vistas, to see and record this extraordinary landscape of mythic dimensions, of the "wine-dark sea," and of the light. What elements are combined alchemically to produce that light I know not. In my travels all over the world it is unparalleled; the way this light reflects upon the whitewashed towns of Greece has given an unending range of subjects for my camera.

There is a plasticity of form in the organic way in which houses are formed, often as if growing out of the rocks. Then, house and rocks are both whitewashed and do become one form to the eye. One can understand how in this land people just took for granted that the gods would come down from Mount Olympus and commingle with mortals.

A great surprise for me was to note that, unlike people in many other cultures, Greeks are pleased to be photographed. "You want to take my picture? *Veveos!* Of course!" I cannot recall anyone saying no.

There are many who will readily point out that my view of Greece is idealistic. It does not show things as they really are. I can only say to them that there are many realities. I do not choose to focus my camera or my energy on those aspects of twentieth-century culture that have torn the fabric of the Greek tapestry I am attempting to record. It is still possible to go to Greece and find it the way it is seen herein, even in the most popular tourist spots. You may be required to rise at dawn, see those incredible sunrises, and wander the streets before the T-shirts and postcards are hung out for the tourists disembarking from their cruise ships. But it is still there for those who have eyes to see.

Kalo taxidi! (Good journey!)
Barry Brukoff
January 1998

FIROSTEFANI, SANTORINI

INTRODUCTION

"Everything here speaks now, as it did centuries ago, of illumination....
Here the light penetrates directly to the soul, opens the door and windows of the heart, makes one naked,
exposed, isolated in a metaphysical bliss which makes everything clear without being known."
—Henry Miller, *The Colossus of Maroussi*

To know Greece well, Henry Miller once suggested, would take more than a lifetime, but to fall in love with it takes only an instant. The photographs in this book show why: they are images captured by a passionate pilgrim who has fallen in love with the faces, the stones, the light and shadows of the country. Thanks to Barry Brukoff's ability to peer into the beating heart of Greece, even an armchair tourist can fall in love with it, too.

To a Greek, an icon (literally "image") is a window through which he can communicate directly with a saint or divinity. The images in this book are similarly icons through which the observer can learn the reality of Greece and the Greeks—a reality far more complicated and interesting than the familiar sights on the travel posters.

As you may suspect by now, this is not going to be a dispassionate book. It is an ardent portrait of the country in words and images by two men who have found more to admire and marvel at with every journey there.

I was born in a small mountain village on the northern border of the country in 1939 at the beginning of ten years of war. At the age of nine, I and my four sisters left Greece as refugees to join the father I had never met in America, after my mother was executed for planning our escape from the Communist guerrillas occupying our village. The last time I saw her alive, she warned us to throw a black stone behind us when we left, a charm to ensure that we would never return. She was thinking of the famine, war, and hardship that had plagued our mountains.

We left the stone, but the vow not to return was one I couldn't keep, for, as I wrote in the book *Eleni,* "The isolation and cruelty of the landscape made the peasants short-tempered and sometimes drove them mad...but those who managed to escape from these mountains would never find any other place as beautiful."

In 1963, when I finished college and managed to put together enough money, I returned to Greece for the first time as an adult. Since then I've gone back regularly, sometimes four or five times a year, and each time I retrace the path to my village of Lia, perched among the mountain peaks in the northwestern province of Epirus.

Love of country is a major chord in every Greek's character, and the pain of *xenitia*—living away from the native land—is the subject of many sad songs sung by Greeks of the diaspora. Like Antaeus, the giant who lost his great strength when he was not touching the earth, the Greek who lives far from his country is in pain until he can return to his roots. There is a saying: "The most painful experiences a Greek can know are to be an orphan, to be alone, to be in love, and to be away from Greece. And to be away from Greece is the worst of all."

Barry Brukoff was not born Greek, but he has visited the country eighteen times in the last twenty years, investigating its most remote corners and taking thousands of pictures on every visit. He has slept in unheated monastic cells on Mount Athos in order to photograph the religious treasures and ascetic life of its monasteries. He has photographed the columns of the Parthenon at every hour of the day and night, capturing images so unlike the standard postcard views that they present this triumph of the human spirit from a new perspective, as if seen for the first time. In remote Greek villages, he makes a practice of rising with the sun to capture the first stirrings of activity as the fishermen sail out in their boats, the shopkeepers set out their wares, and the housewives carry their pans of food to the large ovens of the local *fourno* in preparation for the midday meal.

Greece is never dull and never what you expect it to be. Everyone knows about the glories of Greek history and culture, but not everyone knows about the endless variety of its landscape. Every curve in the road brings a surprise: sleepy coves and mysterious caverns filled with stalactites and stalagmites, groves of dusty green olive trees, twisted like figures in agony, and dizzying mountain ranges draped in pine and crowned by snow. There is the Vikos Gorge, like a miniature Grand Canyon, and the otherworldly needles of rock topped by monasteries which jut out of the plains of Meteora. There are the vertiginous

villages of Santorini, with its black sand beaches, clinging to the side of the volcano that may have swallowed ancient Atlantis, and there's Metsovo, with its ski chalets, quaintly costumed shepherds, and wild mountain goats, looking like some Alpine village. Like Shakespeare's Cleopatra, Greece seduces her admirers with her infinite variety.

Beyond the beauty of the landscape is the unique light of Greece, like a spotlight trained by the gods on the earth, giving the most humble object or face what Henry Miller described as an "eternal cast." In the stark light of the Greek sun, colors become so pure and clear that they are almost audible, but never brash and glaring. Every patch of color glows with a great subtlety of shades. I know of no other land where shadows really are purple and lavender and a dozen other colors as well. Watching a patch of sea go through its repertory of greens and blues can keep one spellbound for hours.

Greece's unearthly, spiritual, almost holy light is a photographer's dream, and Barry Brukoff has used it to convey the great significance it lends to every scene, stripping an object naked and revealing it to the eye with total honesty. No one can come away from experiencing this light without being profoundly moved, and these photographs convey that mystical quality of the landscape.

The images are also windows into the heart and soul of modern Greece which few tourists see, overwhelmed by the welter of postcard views, pre-packaged archaeological sites, and fake folk art. Our intent is to show the truth of Greece; to share what we've learned about the countryside and the people who live there all year around, tilling the soil or fishing, working in a restaurant or factory during the day, dining out with friends and family at the local *tavernas* at night and dancing at the *bouzoukia* into the late hours.

We ventured inland to the isolated villages and regional towns where most Greeks are born and raised, because there, and not in the frantic urban rush of Athens or Salonika, is where one finds the true Greek character and the overwhelming Greek hospitality.

I was born in a small village—Lia—only an hour's drive from the main port in Epirus, not far from the international sophistication of Corfu and the picturesque minarets of the city of Ioannina, but my village is another world, seemingly untouched by the present. When it rains, the clouds form below us. From any vantage point, the mountains and foothills stretch into the distance like the billows of a grayish purple sea. There is no sign of man and his technology in the view, only the occasional distant church or chapel alone on a hill. As the sun sets, the sound of bells reverberates through the mountainside,

heralding the return of the flocks of goats followed by elderly black-clad shepherds and shepherdesses. The timberline ends above us and beyond that, on the highest peak, are the ruins of a Hellenistic acropolis and an area the villagers still call the *agora* (marketplace) although no one goes there but wild boar and goats.

The past is a living presence in Greece, especially in my village, which has been crossed by every invader, from Romans, Slavs, and Turks to, in my lifetime, Italians, Germans, and Albanians. Antiquities proliferate in our soil. Recently a man from a nearby village, digging a foundation for a garage, found a tomb filled with gold jewelry from the Hellenistic era. There are grave tumuli in my village that I'm sure contain similar treasures.

Until we brought my mother's remains to America, to be buried beside my father, they rested with the bones of our ancestors in the ancient church of St. Demetrios. Just above that church are the ruins of the house where we slept on straw mats near the fireplace, with our sheep and goats sheltered in the basement below. After the Germans burned most of our village, my grandfather rebuilt his house and found in the burned foundations an ancient Roman sword and a coin bearing the profile of Alexander the Great.

Every time I return to my birthplace, I climb up to the Viro—the spring where my mother and the other women would gather to wash their laundry while we children played nearby. Sitting beside the spring, I look up at the acropolis where the soldiers of King Pyrrhus lit signal fires—one of a chain of fires that could send messages deep into Illyria. Whenever I return to my village and see the acropolis above me and the waves of foothills stretching south and west toward the sea, I understand what it is to be Greek—part of a continuous river of history as vital today as it was when the young Alexander recited his school lessons not far from here, under the stern gaze of his tutor, Aristotle.

Goethe wrote: "Of all peoples, the Greeks have dreamt the dream of life best." This book is a celebration of that dream. It is what Greeks call a *meze*—an aperitif to pique the appetite and awaken the yearning to experience more; an invitation to go there and partake in the endless feast that has fulfilled the senses for so many visitors over the centuries.

THE OLD TOWN OF RHODES

THE LAND, THE SEA, AND THE LIGHT

"You should see the landscape of Greece. It would break your heart."
—Lawrence Durrell, *Spirit of Place*

The soil of Greece is dusty, dry, and unpromising, covered with stones and scrub pine clinging to mountain cliffs. The land is a hard taskmaster to those who try to scratch crops from it, yet this red Attic soil produced the richest flowering of civilization the world has ever known. It seems an unlikely miracle, yet when you walk among the stones of Greece and experience the unique combination of light, water, and earth, it all becomes inevitable. No other land could have produced such a people, and this land could have produced nothing else.

There are no harsh extremes in the Greek landscape, no towering Alps. Nature built Greece on a human scale, and the people followed suit, creating their gods and designing their temples to a human scale. This idea of human proportion as the basic unit completely pervades Greek thought.

Less than a quarter of Greece is arable, and only one-tenth of it is good land—primarily in two great fertile plains. The Amphissan plain stretches away from the cliffs of Delphi to the sea in a silvery gray-green carpet of gnarled olive trees. The plain of Thessaly, a dusty gold mosaic of crops, is bounded on the northwest by the sheer, dreamlike cliffs of Meteora, where monasteries cling to the peaks like eagles. The rest is the red, dry, unforgiving soil. The farmer pries the stones from his field and digs terraces to keep the earth from washing downhill. Finding enough water for his crops is a daily battle. Nevertheless, the olives, figs, grapes, wheat, beans, and tobacco that the land provides are not enough to support the Greek people, and food must be imported.

Islands make up one-fifth of the land area of Greece—over fourteen hundred of them, many as bare and gray as the shells of giant turtles floating on the water. The largely mountainous mainland is pocketed with small villages that hang precariously, ready to spill into the valleys. Cypresses like candles, and firs, myrtles, and fig trees grow on the mountainsides, and in the spring there are poppies like drops of blood and heather for the bees. Not much else can flourish here, except for the hardy mountain goats and, in the north, wild boar.

The landscape can be divided into three elements: water, land, and light. Each has almost mystical significance. Take water (*neró*). Knock on the door of the poorest hut in the most remote province of Greece and its inhabitant, before asking your name, will serve you a glass of water accompanied by the traditional sweet. Natural springs are cherished. Villages grow up around them, and for village women, the well or spring is the center of life, as in biblical times. There they share gossip as they fill large clay urns or, more recently, plastic bottles in fluorescent colors, which some still carry home balanced gracefully on their heads.

KASTORIA

Many springs have a history that begins with a legend. In my village, high on a mountainside just below the border of Albania, a stone bench has been placed by a spring beneath an ancient plane tree. Here, according to village legend, Saint Kosmas stopped to drink two hundred years ago, before proceeding over the mountain to his martyrdom.

Some springs are magical. One in Delphi imparts eloquence to the drinker. On the flower-drifted flank of Mount Hymmetus, just outside Athens, an ancient spring bubbles out of the head of a stone ram built into the side of a Byzantine monastery. Any fine Sunday brings Athenian families to picnic in the shade of the old cypresses and to fill containers with the spring's water, celebrated for its ability to enhance fertility.

From a glass of water to the village well to the sea, water has dictated the quality of Greek life throughout history. A Greek is never more than a day's walk from the sight of the ocean. It was by sea that the first inhabitants came and by sea that the island dwellers left home to seek their fortunes because the land could not support them. Greek mariners, from the Argonauts to the shipowners of today, succeeded so well that there are now half as many Greeks living outside the country as the ten million still here.

It is often said that the basic colors of Greece are those of its flag: blue and white. The blue of sea and sky are vivid and ever-changing, and the sun bleaches stones, marble columns, and whitewashed huts to an eye-dazzling incandescence. But there is a third basic color to Greece: the dusty brick-red of the soil. It is everywhere: the bare dirt, the tiled roofs of the little white houses, the dust on the farmer's hands, and the graceful figures of youths and maidens on ancient Greek urns.

The land of Greece may be poor, but it is heartbreakingly beautiful. Nature has carved it into curving bays, dramatic coves, caves with iridescent walls. There are gently rolling hills, snow-topped mountain ranges, beaches of oval white pebbles, sheer needles of rock shot with veins of marble, and flat fields dotted with golden-fleeced sheep.

The Greek has always been sensitive to the beauty of his land. Whenever you round a bend to discover a high cliff or mountain peak in a setting of great drama, you will almost always find a ruined pagan temple or a Byzantine church or monastery built there, to take advantage of the prospect.

SKYROS

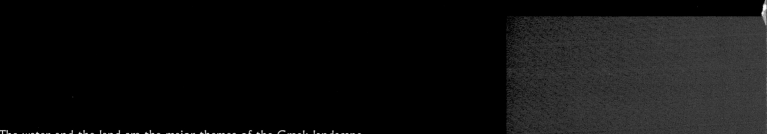

The water and the land are the major themes of the Greek landscape.

Travelers through the ages have struggled to describe this remarkable Greek light, which plays havoc with photographers' film and light meters. My own first impression of the light of Greece was that the air had disappeared. It was as if I had always been conscious of a haze, a refraction caused by the air standing between me and the world. Now that haze was gone.

Two lines from William Blake suggest why the light seems to invest the most humble objects with an eternal cast, a great significance, like something in a drug-induced dream: "If the doors of perception were cleansed, / Everything would appear to man as it is, infinite."

Such words inevitably bring to mind Plato's famous allegory of the cave. He suggested that we on earth are like a man chained in a cave, facing the wall, able to see only the shadows of passing figures and assuming that the shadows are the real objects. Just as each shadow is only a pale reflection of the true thing behind it, Plato believed, every object on earth is a pale reflection of its ideal.

Seeing the intensity of the Greek light, which tolerates no half-tones, no secrets, setting every object ablaze with significance, is the cornerstone to understanding Greece. The ancient Greeks found it natural to discover metaphysical meanings in everyday objects and to personify abstract concepts in physical form. Apollo was the personification of light and of learning. In Hellenistic times, every stream and tree harbored the spirit of a naiad or a nymph. Today, the most unlettered Greek still senses the god behind the man, the eternal truth behind the most humble object. He looks at the earth, the sea, the sun, and sees infinity.

In the pure light of Greece, a simple wooden chair with a frayed, caned seat sits empty, awaiting the arrival of its daily occupant: a leathery-skinned peasant, who will come to the *taverna*, clicking his worry beads in his hand, eager to debate the political news from today's newspaper. He will pass hours drinking tiny cups of thick coffee, challenging his cronies to hard-fought games of *tavli* and passionate arguments about the state of the world. He will drink *raki* and wax philosophical—feeling himself no less qualified than Socrates to expound on the gnarlier questions of life, death, philosophy, and religion. At the end of the day the peasant/philosopher will climb back up the mountain to his evening meal and his hearth, leaving the chair empty until the morrow.

In the divine light of Greece that chair, etched by the sun against the rough whitewashed wall of the *taverna*, is not just a chair but an eloquent testament to the cycles of Greek life, speaking of the slow passage of days and generations throughout the centuries since the earth mother, Gaea, gave birth to a race of giants when the world was young.

NAFPAKTOS HARBOR

MOLIVOS, LESBOS
Overleaf: MYKONOS

MYKONOS

SKIATHOS

PATMOS

800-YEAR-OLD OLIVE TREES, PARGA

ANDRITSENA

EDESSA

TINOS

KYTHIRA

Overleaf: HYDRA

MONEMVASIA

FROM DIONYSIOU MONASTERY, MOUNT ATHOS

CHANIA, CRETE

VATHIA, MANI

SPETSES

PAPINGO

THE ISLAND, IOANNINA

NAXOS

Overleaf: THE PELOPONNESE FROM HYDRA

SKYROS

SKYROS

THE PALAMIDI FORT, NAFPLION

CLASSICAL GREECE

"Where'er we tread, 'tis haunted, holy ground"
—Lord Byron, *Childe Harold's Pilgrimage*

The glory that was Greece is a hard act to follow. It would be wrong to approach the country as a museum, a shrine to a dead civilization. Those who come to worship the ancient Greeks and gaze only at their temples miss the dynamic, creative civilization of today. Nevertheless, the legacy of the classical Greeks, who reached the pinnacle of human knowledge, art, and architecture five centuries before Christ, cannot be ignored, because they have left their footprints everywhere.

A farmer plows his field and unearths coins bearing the face of Alexander the Great. Holiday swimmers glimpse huge amphorae lying on the ocean floor, testament to the time when Greece was the shopping center of the world. Sometimes the sea even gives back a priceless bronze statue like the Zeus discovered in the 1920s off Cape Artemisium and the two heroic figures of warriors from wrecks off the shores of southern Italy, found in 1972. When the city of Athens set out to expand the subway system recently, work had to be stopped every few weeks because another legendary site had been unearthed, such as the Dimosio Sima cemetery, where war heroes, possibly including Pericles himself, were buried. Byron was right: the Greek earth is filled with ghostly reminders of the ancient Greeks and their triumphs.

The achievements of Greece in the fifth century before Christ were so extraordinary and inexplicable that the flowering of this small country is often referred to as the Greek miracle. It began with a vision that arose in the city of Athens on the dusty plains of Attica and exploded over the Western hemisphere like the birth of a new sun. It seemed a revolutionary and dangerous idea in a world where animal gods, brutal tyrants, and the omnipotent pharaohs of Egypt ruled the most advanced civilizations. This unprecedented idea, born in Greece, has warmed and illuminated us ever

since, sometimes obscured by shadows, then bursting forth anew as it did when our own nation was created on the model of the original.

This vision—the Greek idea—was that society functions best if all citizens are equal and free to shape their lives and share in running their state—in a word, democracy.

With its birth came an explosion of the creative spirit in Greece, producing the architecture, the art, the drama, and the philosophy that have shaped Western civilization ever since. "What was then produced in art and thought has never been surpassed, and very rarely equalled," wrote the classicist Edith Hamilton, "and the stamp of it is on all the art and all the thought of the Western world."

Today it's hard for us to realize exactly how radical an idea it was: individual freedom. No society before the Greeks had ever thought that equality and freedom of the individual could lead to anything but disaster. It took the small and unimpressive city-state of Athens, twenty-five centuries ago, to suggest that individual freedom and order are not incompatible.

The Greeks understood very well that unlimited freedom can produce chaos. But they came to believe that if people were given freedom and chose to impose limits on it through laws they enacted themselves, order could be achieved without despotism. The faith of Greeks in every individual's unique capacity to reason and to impose self-control from within was a major force in creating that peculiar Athenian experiment—the world's first democracy—which involved every farmer, shepherd, and tradesman in the government. "The individual can be trusted," Pericles said. "Let him alone."

Mortal man became the standard by which things were judged and measured. Buildings were built to accommodate the body and please the eye of a man, not a giant. Gods were portrayed as resembling human beings, not animals, monsters, or fantastic creatures with multiple arms, eyes, and breasts. And the ruler—the lawmaker and judge—was for the first time the ordinary citizen. As Sophocles wrote in *Antigone:* "Wonders are there many—none more wonderful than man."

It was no coincidence that the Greek discovery of individual worth and freedom produced the most profound advances in art and sculpture, architecture, drama, and philosophy. If the spark of divinity is to be found in man, then the form and appearance of man would inevitably be the proper subject matter of the artist.

An artist who believes that there is "none more wonderful than man" will make the human form his object of study and will create gods in the image of man. Although no paintings remain, the few great Classical sculptures that survive demonstrate that Classical Greece produced a flowering of artistic skill that has never been equaled in the twenty-five centuries since.

When reason and spirit fuse, as they did in the Classical Age, the natural goal of the artist is to portray beauty in the image of man, but idealized. Like the philosopher and scientist, the artist sought the essence of the thing—trying to strip away confusing details and variations to uncover the purest ideal of the human body, the perfect balance between flesh, spirit, and intellect. No symbols or special trappings of divinity were required beyond the figure's physical harmony. The most perfect beauty, to the Greek of the fifth century, was the most pure and unadorned, as the Parthenon is the most beautiful and harmonious, yet most simple building ever made.

Within an incredibly short period of time, the representation of the human figure achieved its finest expression, idealized yet completely natural, like the bronze Zeus of Artemisium from the mid-fifth century and Praxiteles' fourth-century marble masterpiece, Hermes and the infant Dionysos. With these statues, metal and stone were wrought into the finest representation of the idealized human form ever created by the hand of man. The Greek miracle was complete.

Why did this miracle spring from the soil of Greece rather than a mightier, richer, or more ancient civilization? No one can say for certain. The matchless beauty of the Greek landscape, built on a human scale, may be part of it. Another reason may be that the Greeks lived at the crossroads of three continents, venturing from their land all over the Mediterranean world to trade and establish colonies. Classical Greek cities, the marvels of the ancient world, still lie in ruins in Turkey, Syria, Lebanon, and Iran.

The Greeks had the chance to examine the ideas of other civilizations and compare them to their own. They had the explorer's boldness, the artist's passion for beauty, the philosopher's yearning for basic truths. Ultimately their experiences and instincts led to the creation of democracy, which provided the climate, as historian Michael Grant has noted, "in which the geniuses who created Athenian tragedy, comedy, philosophy and art found it possible to flourish."

The relics of their achievements, battered by the centuries, survive to amaze us still, most visibly on the sacred hill at the heart of Athens.

Many ancient cities had an acropolis ("highest city"), but the Acropolis of Athens, with the Parthenon as its chief treasure, is the most famous. It was a sanctuary to Athena, the virgin goddess (*Parthenos*) and patron of the city. The design and construction of the buildings that still dominate the skyline of the capital were supervised by the great sculptor and architect Phidias.

Seen from any angle, the Parthenon seems to float at the highest point of the Sacred Rock. Its majesty is a kind of optical illusion, achieved by an application of the laws of perspective so sophisticated that succeeding architects have never been able to equal it. The architect created its perfectly linear appearance without using a single straight line. From the slightly convex base to the fluted Doric columns that taper toward the top and lean toward the center, it was designed to attract and beguile the human eye.

Even now, with the colossal gold and ivory statue of the goddess long gone, the walls shattered by the explosion of gunpowder stored inside by the Turks, and the pediments denuded of the reliefs shipped by Lord Elgin to the British Museum in the early nineteenth century, the first sight of the Parthenon, especially by moonlight, fills one with a kind of religious awe. No wonder pilgrims have come to Greece for twenty-five centuries to admire the ruined but eloquent temples of the ancients, from Delphi to Olympia to the Doric temple of Poseidon that crowns the rocky headland of Cape Sounion outside of Athens, where Lord Byron carved his name into one of the fluted columns. Sounion's starkly beautiful ribs of marble, which form a diadem atop one of the world's most dramatic cliffs, have challenged the descriptive powers of writers from Melville to Byron to Rilke and still draw admirers every day to watch as the sun drops behind the temple into the sapphire waters of the bay below.

Such a greatness of architecture, literature, art, philosophy, and government set a standard for all the civilizations that came after. For nearly a century, on the austere plain of Attica, mind and spirit existed in equilibrium as never before or since, and the eloquent ruins that remain demonstrate for all eternity the heights to which the human spirit can soar.

THE AMPHITHEATER AT SUNSET, DELOS

KNOSSOS, CRETE

THE ANCIENT CITY OF KORINTH

THE GREAT DOOR, TEMPLE OF APOLLO, NAXOS

THE TEMPLE OF POSEIDON, CAPE SOUNION

THE HERMES OF PRAXITELES, OLYMPIA

FULL MOON ECLIPSE OVER THE PARTHENON, ATHENS

OLYMPIA

THE BYZANTINE WORLD

"While the West was slumbering though the night of the early Middle Ages, bereft of learning,
of organized civil life and tradition, Byzantium remained the sole repository of the glories of Greece and Rome."
—René Guerdan, *Byzantium*

The two great veins of culture that flowed together to produce modern Greece and even Western civilization are ancient Greece and Byzantium. In 330 A.D., the Emperor Constantine, the first Roman emperor to convert to Christianity, moved his capital from Rome to an old Greek city on the Bosporus called Byzantion. It was renamed Constantinople in his honor and remained the center of the Eastern Roman Empire for more than a thousand years, long after the fall of Rome.

During the arid centuries of the Dark Ages, it was the scholars, monks, and artists of Byzantium who cherished Greek culture and kept Western civilization alive, finally carrying their art and knowledge back to the West after the fall of Constantinople in 1453. Fleeing the invading Turks, they landed in Italy to ignite the first sparks of the Renaissance.

For a time after the founding of Constantinople there were two emperors and two empires: the Eastern and Western Roman Empires, symbolized by the two-headed eagle that was a universal motif. The people of the East called themselves Romans, but they spoke Greek and admired ancient Greek art, literature, and philosophy. The new Christian thinkers in Constantinople skillfully incorporated Greek philosophical ideas into their ideology, even though the "pagan" schools of Plato and Aristotle had been closed. In the Eastern Empire, art and architecture developed distinctive new forms that were usually rigid and two-dimensional, yet strangely haunting and beautiful.

After the Western Roman Empire began to crumble in the fifth century under the onslaught of barbarian invaders, the Eastern Roman Empire—Byzantium—flourished and grew to include parts of southern and eastern Europe, northern Africa, and the Middle East. While its administration was Roman, its language and culture remained Greek. For the next millennium, Byzantine Greeks preserved the heritage of their ancestors, expressing their own mystical artistic vision in brilliant mosaics, icons, illuminated manuscripts, and liturgical music and spreading literacy and religion to new corners of the world, including Russia. Historian Charles Diehl summarized Byzantium this way: "The champion of Christendom against Islam, the defender of civilization against barbarism and educator of the Slavic East."

The most visible achievements of the Byzantine Empire today are its domed churches, usually plain on the outside but encrusted inside with frescoes, mosaics, highly stylized murals, and icons, shimmering with gold and the colors of jewels. The church's plain exterior was meant to represent the daily world, but the interior, gleaming with saints and angels and dominated by the all-seeing face of Christ the Pantocrator gazing down from the dome, represented the ideal or spiritual universe. The worshiper standing in the church, gazing at the icon wall of saints and angels guarding the holy of holies, couldn't help feeling awed and uplifted, as if he had entered the portals of heaven.

Although Byzantine artists were influenced by the artistic traditions of ancient Greece, their focus was spiritual and mystical, resulting in flat, two-dimensional figures designed on abstract patterns to emphasize their holiness. The usually anonymous artist was required by the Church to follow very specific formulas when portraying holy figures. Icons were and are considered sacred. Each iconographer who painted a holy figure had to follow the design and colors of his predecessors as closely as possible.

Even today Orthodox Christians believe that an icon is a kind of window between earth and heaven through which the inhabitants of heaven have chosen to reveal themselves. There are many legends of icons that miraculously appeared, "not made by hands." Some images, especially of Christ, were believed to have been painted originally by the apostle Luke.

In the churches, ancient and venerated icons are often covered in precious metals to protect them from the lips of the worshipers and are sometimes studded with gems. The faithful come to seek intervention and favors from the saints and often hang on the icons jewelry, coins, and votive figures (*filakta*) symbolizing their wishes.

The Eastern and Western branches of the Christian Church split in 1054 and developed in different directions. The Western Church of Rome evolved toward scholasticism, while the Eastern branch received a strong infusion of mysticism. The Eastern Orthodox Church of today, led by the Patriarch in Constantinople, the spiritual leader of 300 million Orthodox Christians throughout the world, is in many ways the most similar in practices and beliefs to the primitive Christian Church. It has remained remarkably unchanged over the centuries by hiding and isolating its clergy from the many invaders who threatened it—Arabs, Turks, Mongols, even Christian Crusaders from the West. The surviving churches and monasteries became ghettos of conservatism, fighting to preserve the old faith.

led. Those who reached Italy brought their precious scrolls and manuscripts with them and their infusion of ancient Greek thought would eventually drive back the shadows of the Dark Ages to create the Renaissance.

In other countries, however, especially Greece, the clergy barricaded themselves in churches built on the most isolated and inaccessible cliffs. The incredible monasteries of Meteora, for example, which still make the traveler shake his head in disbelief, cling to rocks so sheer that the monks could not leave or receive supplies except by lowering large baskets on ropes to the plains far below. Orthodox monks and nuns, unlike some Roman Catholic orders, are devoted chiefly to asceticism and mysticism rather than missionary efforts, teaching, and social work. In northern Greece, travelers can still see caves high in the cliffs that were occupied by hermits—anchorite monks whose only contact with civilization was a rope by which they would haul up food and supplies left by the faithful.

The unique area of Mount Athos, fifteen monasteries clinging to a steep, rocky promontory in Macedonia overlooking the Aegean Sea, today houses about fifteen hundred monks. Life on the Holy Mountain, an autonomous republic within the Greek state, has scarcely changed in centuries, although the population has dwindled. The monks' days pass in prayer and meditation, and no females—not even female animals—have ever been allowed to enter the sacred precincts.

For more than a thousand years, the monks of Mount Athos have lived lives of self-denial and austerity amidst fabulous treasures of Byzantine art. Their goal is to free themselves of the temptations of the world and achieve

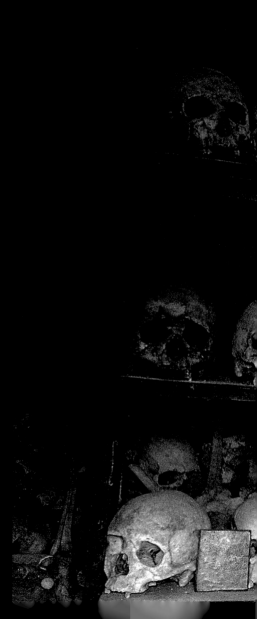

OSSUARY, MONASTERY OF THE TRANSFIGURATION, METEORA

METEORA

In Greece, the Church permeates every layer of life. A Greek's year is based on the festivals of the Church calendar and he is feted not on his birthday, but on the day of the saint for which he was named. When any endeavor, such as the building of a new house, is begun, the priest is asked to say a blessing on the spot. When a Greek has a problem, he will go to church and light a candle to the saint most likely to hear his prayers and intercede in the matter. Every event of the year—the sowing of crops, the first voyage of the village fishing fleet, the first fruits of the harvest—is marked with an appropriate religious ceremony. Thousands of the ailing and the devout travel yearly to the island of Tinos, especially on the Virgin Mary's holiday, August 15, to worship a miraculous icon of the Virgin and pray for a cure, some crawling on their knees from the ship's dock up the steps to the church to demonstrate their piety.

Crossing himself for luck or spitting to ward off the Evil Eye, a Greek invokes his religion many times a day. Most Greek homes have a family shrine in the eastern corner holding icons and a candle or oil lamp that is tended daily. The country is studded with chapels and tiny roadside shrines, some no bigger than a birdhouse, built in thanksgiving for services rendered or in memory of someone who died nearby. These are often situated at the most picturesque bends in the road, just as the ancient Greeks built shrines to pagan gods in the same spots. They provide the traveler with a chance for rest and prayerful meditation. Devout passersby will fuel the lamps, tend the wicks, and perhaps leave a contribution for the upkeep of the shrine.

It's not surprising that religion is so important in Greece. During the four hundred years of occupation, until the Turkish yoke was finally thrown off in 1821, there was only the Church to provide Greeks with a sense of unity and national identity. The Byzantine music, art, literature, and oral history that survived were conserved by the priests and the monks. To learn to read and write their own language, Greek children were sent to "secret schools" surreptitiously run by the clergy at night. Today, every Greek child knows a nursery song that asks the moon to light his steps to his lessons in the darkness "so that I may learn letters, the things of God." Without the Church to protect and teach them during the centuries of Turkish occupation, Greeks would have lost their art, music, literature, and all the traces of their heritage. And without Byzantium to cherish and safeguard the art, literature, and wisdom of the ancients, those earlier triumphs of man's mind and spirit would have been lost to the world forever.

MONASTERIES OF THE TRANSFIGURATION AND VARLAAM

ROUSANNOU MONASTERY, METEORA

ROUSANNOU MONASTERY, METEORA

MISTRAS

THESSALONIKI

XENOFONTOS MONASTERY, MOUNT ATHOS

XENOFONTOS MONASTERY, MOUNT ATHOS

XENOFONTOS MONASTERY, MOUNT ATHOS

DOCHEIARIOU MONASTERY, MOUNT ATHOS

XENOFONTOS MONASTERY, MOUNT ATHOS

DIONYSIOU MONASTERY, MOUNT ATHOS

THESSALONIKI

GREAT LAVRA MONASTERY, MOUNT ATHOS

XENOFONTOS MONASTERY, MOUNT ATHOS

THE PEOPLE

"The Greeks of today may have little direct affinity with the Greeks of antiquity…. But the same environment has bred them, and the same ideas have turned them into a nation."
—Lord Kinross, *Greece*

The famous ancient Greek statues like Praxiteles' Hermes and the Venus de Milo have created such vivid images of what Greeks *should* look like that it may come as a shock to discover that many inhabitants of the country today are short, squat, and dark rather than tall and blond with a godlike brow and a nose that springs straight from the forehead. On further acquaintance, however, modern Greeks begin to look more familiar. There's Plato in a coffeehouse, arguing politics in a Socratic dialogue. There's Odysseus daringly navigating rush hour traffic in Constitution Square on a motorbike. There's Penelope sitting behind a typewriter, while hopeful suitors wait for her coffee break. Instead of igniting another Trojan War, the beautiful Helen is a newsreader on television or a contestant in the Miss World pageant. In every harbor leathery-skinned Argonauts set out at dawn, eager to risk the temptations of the sirens' songs.

Every Greek home holds joy and tragedy straight out of Aeschylus, Sophocles, and Euripides. Behind the olive skin of the modern Greek beats the heart and the spirit of the ancients: the same restless curiosity, shrewdness, love of adventure, and the same capacity for suffering. With his ancestors he shares the tendency to use strong words and violent gestures, and is blessed with the same warm heart, disdain for time, and delight in life lived fully, with all the senses awake.

There are still Greeks whose physical features are hauntingly like those in the museums. They are found especially in remote villages that escaped foreign incursions. But the Greeks of today are not the children of the Greeks who first saw the tragedies of Sophocles and Euripides. Modern Greeks carry on their faces the tale of invasions by the Turks, Slavs,

Franks, and Italians. Greek character, however, has survived centuries of foreign rule intact. More than most Europeans, Greeks are still close to the basic springs of character formation: land and climate. "Even if the Greeks are annihilated and only one Greek is left," said the writer Pericles Giannopoulos, "he'll teach the conquerors Greek and make Greeks of them. The earth, the stones, the mountains are Greek and make Greeks."

To survive despite the country's harsh terrain and struggling economy requires a strong heart and a shrewd mind. Every Greek is as much pragmatist as poet; both artist and artisan, because he cannot get by any other way. Throughout history they have led this double life. An ancient Greek considered himself a battlefield where Apollo's reason and Dionysos' passions struggled for control.

The modern Greek sees this inner battle as one fought between the two sides of his nature, the *Hellene* and the *Romios.* The average Greek is certain that there flows in his veins some of the blood of his noble ancestors, but he is just as certain that he harbors plenty of baser characteristics inherited from the invaders who followed. When he feels altruistic, courageous, or creative, he calls himself a *Hellene,* the word for Greek that was used even before Pericles' time. When he feels devious, obstinate, or selfish, he calls himself a *Romios,* which is the Greek word for Roman. The part of him that is searching the stars is Hellenic, the part fighting for position in the dirt is Romaic.

This schism goes back to the Byzantine era. After Constantinople fell to the Turks, all subjects under Ottoman rule, including those in Greece, called themselves by the word *Romios,* meaning a citizen of the Byzantine Empire or New Rome. During four centuries of subjugation, Greeks had to use all the strength, cunning, and deviousness they could muster. After winning independence in 1831, the Greeks self-consciously tried to return to their ancient greatness and encourage qualities that they considered Hellenic, but every step of the way, they have had to fight the Romaic side of their nature, which focuses on the real world, money, and power, relies on instinct, distrusts and tries to bypass the law, values learning as a means to advancement, loves folk music and dance, and feels strong loyalty to their native region. The Romios will consider any compromise to gain personal ends. The Hellenic side, in contrast, focuses on the ideal, relies on logic, respects the law, prefers European music and dance, and would rather debate philosophy than barter for tonight's dinner.

The main characteristic shared equally by the Romaic and the Hellenic sides of the Greek is a passionate love of country. During World War II, the Greeks fought as fiercely and as courageously against the Italians and the Germans as their ancestors had against the Persians twenty-five centuries earlier. In the autumn of 1940, when Italian troops poured over the border, a vastly outnumbered Greek army drove them out of the country and back across half of Albania, humiliating Mussolini in the eyes of the world. This forced Hitler to divert forces to the south and delay his invasion of Russia, which some historians see as a turning point in the war.

LINDOS, RHODES

The most sacred virtue and duty to a Greek is hospitality, which in Greek is *philoxenia,* a word that can be translated as "love of strangers." (The Greek word *xenos* means both foreigner and guest.) Because a traveler in Greece has always been at the mercy of the harsh land, the tradition of hospitality took root in antiquity. A family would slaughter its only hen to feed the stranger who knocked at the door. In the ancient tragedies, a breach of hospitality called down the severest punishments from the gods. Like many traditions bred of necessity and good sense, *philoxenia* can get out of hand on occasion and Greeks have been known to come to blows in an argument over who gets to pick up the check.

Greeks are not only hospitable to strangers, they have a lively curiosity which may show itself in questions about their guests' most personal affairs. A stranger's income, sex life, politics, religion—all are considered grist for dinner table conversation. The curiosity of Greeks is equaled by their sense of humor, as essential a spice to their conversation as oregano is to their food. Greek humor can have a cutting edge, and competitive repartee—a verbal one-upmanship—is a popular pastime. More rarely, Greeks will turn the joke on themselves, much as Socrates joked about the shape of his nose and the bad temper of his wife.

A Greek tends to be convinced of his own omniscience on any subject. After readily admitting his limited education and experience, he will proceed to explain why he is right and everyone else is wrong. Every Greek is an Aristotle, and his particular area of expertise is usually politics. There are almost as many shades of political thought in Greece as there are degrees of sweetness to the tiny cups of coffee which inevitably accompany the debate. (According to purists, there are thirty-six different shades of sweetness from *schetos*—black—to *vari glikos*—very sweet.)

When two men are seen arguing in a *kafenion,* shouting, swearing, and making threatening gestures, a stranger may fear that blood is about to be spilled, but chances are this is just an animated conversation about the day's political news or the relative merits of Greece's rival soccer teams: Olympiakos and Panatheniakos. The Greek flair for drama can also be seen at any minor traffic accident, when nearby drivers abandon their vehicles and rush to the scene for an excited discussion of who's at fault, delivering judgment in the time-honored tradition of the ancient Greek chorus. And in any village *plateia* or urban street market, a gaggle of black-clad Greek widows is certain to be found, sitting on their haunches to discuss with the wisdom of the chorus the affairs of friends and neighbors, usually concluding their reports of some family's misdeeds with the observation that the apple doesn't fall far from the tree.

The primary arbiters of social behavior are the extended family and the community. Greece has the lowest rate of violent crime in Europe, and social scientists attribute this to the fact that there is little anonymity except in the cities and, even there, family and community ties are still very strong. The misbehavior of one family member is seen to besmirch the entire *soi* or clan. In Greece extended families usually live together, and the elders are respected and expected to care for and teach the youngest. Greeks view with equal contempt the thought of putting the aged in a nursing home or hiring an outsider as a babysitter.

In any discussion of the Greek character, the power of popular culture inevitably brings to mind the irrepressible *Zorba the Greek* of Nikos Kazantzakis and Melina Mercouri's hooker with the heart of gold from *Never on Sunday*. Like all stereotypes, these have become clichés, but both characters illustrate an important element in the Greek nature called *kefi*. The word indicates a zest for life, an enthusiasm that can make a man rise from the table in a *taverna* or nightclub and begin to dance by himself, driven by the plaintive melodies of the bouzouki or clarinet. Onlookers may indicate they share in his *kefi* by hissing or crying *"Opa!"* (To applaud would be an invasion of his private emotions.) As his *kefi* grows, the dancer might be inspired to lift a *taverna* table in his teeth, complete with dishes, or to smash plates on the floor or throw flowers at a singer or performer who has particularly touched his heart.

The greatest thing about the Greeks is that, despite all the hardships of their daily life, despite poverty and many tragic episodes in their recent national history, they always have *kefi*. The smallest occasion or achievement or feast day is a cause for a party, and everyone who passes by will be invited to join. A Yankee friend once remarked to me rather wistfully, "The average Greek has more fun attending a wedding than the average WASP has in a whole lifetime." Edith Hamilton had much the same thought in mind when she wrote in *The Greek Way,* "To rejoice in life, to find the world beautiful and delightful to live in, was a mark of the Greek spirit which distinguished it from all that had gone before. It is a vital distinction."

SKYROS

HERAKLION, CRETE

OIA, SANTORINI

PAROS

ARCHANGELOS, RHODES

FISHERMEN, YOUNG AND OLD, MYKONOS

MYKONOS

NAFPLION

PHAESTOS, CRETE

EPIRUS

CORFU

LINDOS, RHODES

ATHENS

*"There are still Greeks whose
physical features are hauntingly like
those in the museums."*

MYKONOS

METEORA

MYKONOS

ARCHANGELOS, RHODES

LINDOS, RHODES

CORFU

MOLIVOS, LESBOS

MESTA, CHIOS

KALEIDOSCOPE

"Nothing is lacking in Greece; it lies before us, a complete, firmly delineated world,
a self-contained microcosm which includes every basic element of the earth, and all within our range of vision."
—Ioannis Gaitanides *On the Power of the Greek Landscape*

One hundred and eighty years ago, an Englishman created a children's toy out of two slanted mirrors and a tube containing beads and bits of glass that formed colorful patterns as the tube was turned. To name it he combined three Greek words: *kalos*—good or beautiful; *eidos*—shapes; and "scope" from *skopeion*—to look at. Although the fragments inside the toy fall at random, thanks to the replication of the mirrors they create ever-changing symmetrical designs; beautiful shapes worth examining carefully.

All of Greece is a kaleidoscope, endless in variety, never the same from one moment to the next, astonishing the eye at every turn. No matter where you look, you are struck by beauty. In spring, wild mountain slopes in the north of Greece burst into a tapestry of colors: scarlet poppies, white and yellow daisies, mauve heather, and the magenta flowers of the Judas trees. On the southern islands of the Cyclades, piled with white sugar-cube houses, resplendent sunsets send purple shadows bouncing up steep flights of steps as donkeys descend, picking their way home for the night. In every sleepy harbor, fishermen sit cross-legged on the docks, mending their yellow nets as the setting sun bathes the sky blood-red and burgundy before sinking into Homer's aptly described wine-dark sea.

In Greece the intensity of the sun creates deep velvet shadows against the whitewashed walls and intensifies the fanciful colors that villagers use to embellish their doorways and gates—turquoise and lavender, salmon pink and lime green, blood red and sapphire blue. And in every shadow lurks the silhouette of a cat.

AEGINA

PAROS

NAXOS

NAXOS

Cats are the punctuation in the scenes of Greek life. Wherever you are, if you look long enough, you will find them, peering from a balcony, curled up asleep under a *taverna* chair, nursing their young amid the fallen columns of the Acropolis, eyeing intruders with alert attention, and moving on, when they choose to do so, with the liquid grace of dancers. They breed haphazardly: long-eared, long-faced descendants of the sacred cats that were worshiped by the pharaohs. In every cafe or fish restaurant, as soon as the first plate of *mezedakia* is brought to the table, they materialize as if by magic. They await handouts with stoic patience because they are dependent on the kindness of strangers, for few cats in Greece are pampered pets. Nevertheless, during a time of political turmoil and student riots in 1973, I watched black-clad Greek women defy a military curfew every day at considerable personal risk to feed the army of stray cats that lived in a vacant lot across from my Athens apartment.

As if the natural beauty of their country were not enough, the Greeks love to embellish their homes and their most mundane implements. They seem to have an instinctive urge to gild the lily, much as the ancient Greeks lavished their marble statues with jewels, paint, and precious metals. A shepherd will carve his staff (or an old man his walking stick) into fantastic designs of serpents and animals. In the countryside you may see an old crone standing among a flock of sheep, spinning yarn between her fingers from a hank of raw wool attached to her distaff. Looking closer, you'll find that this fork-like implement has been carved into shapes of religious or domestic significance and signed with the initials of the owner.

From childhood, women embroider the linens and weave the blankets for their dowries, stitching images of weddings and celebrations. Those linens are stored in painted wooden *cassellas,* decorated with carvings of churches and cypress trees, flowers and warriors, initials and dates, ready for the moment when the dowry will be placed on a truck, cart, or donkey and paraded through the village behind the newlyweds to their new home. Some grooms still carve by hand the *stephanothiki,* the glass-fronted wooden cabinet used to display the intertwined wedding crowns, like one I bought in Hydra years ago that features an openwork wreath of curling ivy and primitive winged angels, topped by an elaborate cross.

For centuries, in the southern islands and on the mainland, Greeks have decorated the courtyards and walks of their churches and homes with elaborate pebble mosaics, using the various colors of oval stones found on the beaches, polished smooth by the sea. These humble compositions are as eloquent a testament to Greek pride of place and artistic skill as the famous jewel-toned Hellenistic mosaics still visible on the floors of archaeological sites like Delos and Pella.

In Pirgi and other towns on the island of Chios, buildings have always been etched with cubist geometric patterns in paint and plaster that contrast vividly with the red-orange kumquats, a specialty of the island, hanging on the "embroidered" walls to dry. In Greece, even a dovecote is embellished with towers and lacy plaster motifs that make it look more like Cinderella's castle than a home for domestic fowl.

The national passion for decoration is demonstrated by the painted olive oil tins overflowing with red geraniums and the ever-present basil plant outside even the humblest front steps. Basil is not just for cooking in Greece; it has religious significance as well, and even boats and kiosks will usually have a pot of basil tucked somewhere for good luck.

The Greek housewife carefully whitewashes her home and walk at least once a year, to ensure that all will be pristine for Easter. The layers of lime-based white paint build up over time like sugar icing, outlining stairways and streets and gleaming in the moonlight. The housewife crochets lace curtains to hang in the windows, braids the first roses and wildflowers of spring into a May wreath to hang on the front door, and plants her garden with the same eye for beauty that she uses to arrange the food she cooks in elaborate presentations. The men are equally given to artistic expression. The organ grinder's *latérna*, the carriage driver's phaeton, even the truck driver's truck are often covered with masterpieces of folk art: hand-painted portraits, murals, and charms against the Evil Eye.

Even the dead are remembered in surroundings of beauty with gifts of love. The deceased may be buried with a coin on the eyelids or between the lips, to pay Charon, the ferryman to Hades, for his services, and an icon is placed over the heart. If someone dies young, a man is dressed as a groom and a woman in bridal white. At the funeral, the grave is covered with huge, freestanding floral arrangements, often in a horseshoe shape. In the villages, women compose the wailing dirges, the *miroloyia* (words of fate) to honor the person's life. The simple tomb, often built above ground with a removable marble lid, will be decorated with a portrait of the deceased, usually a photograph under glass, and an oil lamp with a bottle of oil so that mourners visiting the grave can light the lamp and say a prayer.

The bereaved hold a memorial service, often including an entire meal, on the fortieth day after death, when the soul of the dead departs. At the funeral and the memorial services, the family distributes *kollyva,* made of boiled wheat cooked with walnuts, almonds, raisins, sugar, cinnamon, and pomegranate seeds, which the mourners eat as a symbol of eternal life.

In many parts of Greece, the bones of the deceased are exhumed by their family after three years and washed in water and wine (an ancient custom predating Alexander the Great). They are placed in a container in the narthex of the church for sanctification, then stored in an ossuary called a *kimitírion* or sleeping place.

All the stages of life from birth to death are embraced and celebrated by the community as public occasions. The Greeks are a gregarious people and the testament to this is the proliferation of chairs everywhere: in restaurants and coffee shops, in alleys, on balconies, along the harborside. The crude, wooden, cane-seated chairs are stacked, piled, gathered in companionable groups, seemingly in perpetual anticipation of a party. There's a saying that a Greek needs four chairs to sit properly: one for each arm and another for a footrest.

ARGOS, PELOPONNESE

Every neighborhood in Greece has a *kafenion,* which the men treat as a social club, even if it's no more than a gaggle of chairs beneath the plane tree in the village square. Watch the arrival of the older and more respected regulars every morning. Each man chooses a table of his own. There he holds court while admirers and petitioners come to pay their respects. Only for a heated political discussion or game of *tavli* will the *eminences grises* of the establishment pull their chairs together at one table.

Cats, chairs, tombstones, and pebble mosaics are all fragments tumbled together in the kaleidoscope to create the ever-changing shapes that are unique to this country. Nature has given Greece an infinite variety of beautiful images from the island villages of spun sugar to the fir-covered mountainous northern villages of stone and wood to the Italianate arcaded streets of Corfu, where the children play English-style rugby around a bandstand, to the brilliant bougainvillea vines climbing the narrow white alleys and staircases of Mykonos.

Greece is a feast for the eyes, never disappointing, always surprising, always exhausting the senses with its gifts. As usual, Lord Byron said it best:

No earth of thine is lost in vulgar mould,

But one vast realm of wonder spreads around,

And all the Muse's tales seem truly told,

Till the sense aches with gazing to behold

The scenes our earliest dreams have dwelt upon.

The Greeks are well aware of the beauty that surrounds them and never fail to celebrate it. The important thing for the visitor is to keep his eyes open so that no turn of the kaleidoscope escapes his notice.

PIRGI, CHIOS

LINDOS, RHODES

AEGINA

"Even the dead are remembered in surroundings of beauty with gifts of love.
The deceased may be buried with a coin on the eyelids or between the lips, to pay
Charon, the ferryman to Hades, for his services, and an icon is placed over the
heart.... The simple tomb, often built above ground with a removable marble lid,
will be decorated with a portrait of the deceased, usually a photograph under glass,
and an oil lamp with a bottle of oil so that mourners visiting the grave can light
the lamp and say a prayer."

HYDRA

FOLLEGANDROS

MYKONOS

SIFNOS

PIRGI, CHIOS

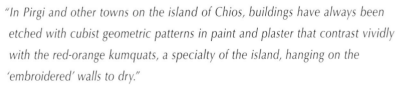
"In Pirgi and other towns on the island of Chios, buildings have always been etched with cubist geometric patterns in paint and plaster that contrast vividly with the red-orange kumquats, a specialty of the island, hanging on the 'embroidered' walls to dry."

ARCHANGELOS, RHODES

"Cats are the punctuation in the scenes of Greek life. Wherever you are, if you look long enough, you will find them,
peering from a balcony, curled up asleep under a taverna chair, nursing their young amid the fallen columns of the Acropolis,
eyeing intruders with alert attention, and moving on, when they choose to do so, with the liquid grace of dancers.
They breed haphazardly: long-eared, long-faced descendants of the sacred cats that were worshiped by the pharaohs.
In every cafe or fish restaurant, as soon as the first plate of mezedakia is brought to the table, they materialize as if by magic."

SPETSES

FIROSTEFANI, SANTORINI

NAXOS

PAROS

MYKONOS

SIMI

MYKONOS

MYKONOS

OIA, SANTORINI

HYDRA

MYKONOS

KALYMNOS

SIFNOS

SKYROS

MYKONOS

THIRA, SANTORINI

NAOUSSA, PAROS

SKOPELOS

"In the pure light of Greece, a simple wooden chair with a frayed, caned seat sits empty, awaiting the arrival of its daily occupant....In the divine light of Greece that chair, etched by the sun against the rough whitewashed wall of the taverna, is not just a chair but an eloquent testament to the cycles of Greek life."

CAPE SOUNION